The little book of

Loss
Loneliness
& Madness

Notes from a survivor

Irene Brankin

Copyright © Irene Brankin 2023
www.irenebrankin.co.uk
First published in the United Kingdom by Irene Brankin

The right of Irene Brankin to be identified as the author of this work has been
asserted by her in accordance with the Copyright, Designs and Patents Act,
1988.
A CIP catalogue record for this book is available from the British Library

ISBN 9798851122002

All rights reserved
No part of this publication may be reproduced, stored in a retrieval system,
transmitted in any form or by any means, electronic, mechanical,
photocopying, recording or otherwise, with the prior permission of the
publishers.

Text and Cover Design by Paula Williams

ACKNOWLEDGMENTS

My love and gratitude to –

Ian, Louise, Lydia and Harry Brankin
The Styles Family
The Mcgreevey Family
The Mccaulay Family
The Morris Family
My Spiruality Group (Joan, Marian, Liz, Jean, Bernadette, John And
Peter)
My Ilfgroup Still Going Strong (Silke, Leigh, Clare, Kim, Yeu-Meng,
Debs, Liz, Teigh-Anne, Anita, Kae)
My Swedish Family of Long-Standing Colleagues
Conn Ritchie – A Man of Depth, Patience and Humour
Helen Ritchie – A Font of Wisdom and Support
My Alpha Group Led by Charles and Barbara McMullen
My Essex Creative Group especially Michael and Michelle
My Essex friends especially Rosemary Cunningham, Mandy Cox
and Jackie (Jay) Ballinger
My next-door neighbours – Shirley, Simon, Noah and Jack
My other next-door neighbours - Carolyn and Jonathan
My two friends, Joan and Barbara, who were godsends
My literary agent – Jacq Burns of London Writers Club
My book designer – Paula Williams

INTRODUCTION

If you have picked up this book, then you've probably lost someone or something really dear to you. Or it may be that you feel bereft, lost, lonely, all sorts of hard and unwelcome feelings that are difficult and painful to bear.

Although everyone feels differently, it may be that you feel people just don't understand. They don't want you to be upset and unwittingly shower you with well-meaning platitudes: 'it'll be alright, things will get better soon.' Or they just want to avoid you. Either way it doesn't feel good. It's haaard.

And right now, you might feel that you will never come out of this lonely place and get on with your life. BUT I am here to tell you that YOU WILL move on when you are ready. Though you might need a loving helping hand to encourage you. I want this book to be that loving, helping hand for you.

All the things you might be experiencing: Loneliness, Loss and Madness – all seem to be taboo subjects that people prefer to dodge or ignore. They are all part of grief. They are all acceptable and normal. They are all connected AND they can be different for all of us.

You might feel excluded from 'normal' life, feel distant from other people and that you don't count.

As you take the loving, helping hand that this book offers, I hope you'll become aware that you do still count. And that you can come through 'Loss, Loneliness and Madness' to be part of life again. And, in your own way, be visible to yourself and re-discover your spark again. It is not all doom and gloom even if it feels like it just now. Watch for that little sliver of light that will come shining through at some point, I promise.

I will be sharing my own personal experience as well as insights over 30 years as a Chartered Counselling Psychologist. This is in the hope you will gain more awareness of what is happening in your experience. And for you to be easier on yourself and what you are going through.

How you might use this book: What I would love for you to do is to take 5 minutes before you start your day to dip into my book, and to reflect on both the questions and answers. You can pick up the book at any stage whatever you are feeling and wherever you are. There is a space, as in a comforting journal, for you to write your own reflections as you move through the book. Remember these pages are for you. May your words be a source of strength and encouragement for you to draw upon when you are ready.

I tend to believe that grief can be like a pressure cooker. It builds up, wants release, can explode, and can do this anywhere unexpectedly. Spending some time easing the pressure for you as you go through your day can be of paramount importance, even if it does not always happen as you would like. Of course, if you were able to choose any time of day that suits you and your lifestyle best would be great.

Whatever loss you have experienced - and there is no judgement about what that is or whether that is large or small or even understood by others - what matters is how the loss has impacted you and your life.

CONTENTS

The book is then split into 6 parts, each one is a key part of helping you work through your loss. And every one of us experiences these to differing degrees.

GRIEF

When I am talking about Grief, I am including that there are different forms of grief and even stages. Mixed in, there is also the matter of regret and guilt. Also, the fact that we don't all grieve the same is important to remember. You might be asking yourself, does it ever go away?

It can be overlooked that grief is a natural effect of loss and is an essential part of life – and of love.

LOSS

I tend to think that loss is a catalyst, and not all losses are the same. We handle them differently, and at varying times in our life.
Our whole identity may be tied up with the person or thing, and that can cause different reactions (usually painful) as we have to face this new identity.

It can leave us at ground zero, and not many of us have been here before.

LONELINESS

In my opinion, at the core of Loneliness is the unmet need of human contact and relationships.

We can feel lonely, even if it's the loss of a pet, a person or circumstance, in the midst of others.

It can be hard to be yourself when lonely, particularly when socialising and the pressure to fit in. Remember Covid, and that lack of touch and connection with others? All can seem unnatural.

MADNESS

Losing our mind can happen because our feelings fluctuate, recover and then bounce down again. It is like life is okay one minute and the next you are fighting away unreality.

We can't just get over it as we can when feeling upset, out of sorts and not quite 'with it'.

Society puts pressure on us to feel happy and be ourselves again, when what we need is to face the reality of our pain, vulnerability and tears. And what about Life's unfairness?

SOME OTHER ISSUES AFFECTING US

People's reactions can vary and are not always supportive at the time. It is quite amazing how we can be ignored and even judged by close friends.

What about your own life and how can you support yourself?
In such a chaotic time, how do you handle these changes?

RECONNECTION

How can you re-connect and come home to you?
Are you able to say 'I See You'?

*'Life is what happens to you
while you are busy making other plans'*

John Lennon

FOREWORD

Who am I to write this book? Because I've experienced all of these aspects of loss and then some.

My husband died in July 2022, when we had moved to Northern Ireland from Essex, England in September, 2019. On top of the crushing loss of my husband, the move also meant that I was away from our home, from friends, and from where I had built up a successful practice. I'd also recently ceased working in mainland Europe, particularly in my beloved Sweden.

We had moved to be nearer to our supportive family - son, daughter-in-law and two lovely grandchildren, in order to draw upon that support. Truly this was great, but as I had lost so much, I was bereft and lonely.

It all became overwhelming. Not only was I grieving, but I was lonely too. And add to that the effects of Lockdown and COVID on my sanity. I really felt I was going mad at times.

I don't know how I stayed afloat, even with the help of my family, and some longstanding friends on Zoom particularly Silke and Leigh, and then I made some new friends, (including the local Newsagent and the Suburban café staff). Thanks also to Shirley, Simon, Barbara, Joan and Conn – my saviours.

Before you read on, I want to say that I'm not able to tell you that you'll be okay in a certain number of months or years as I don't know. Nobody does. The feelings of loss can be there for a lifetime. I can only hope that you will at some point return to yourself (whatever that means for you). That you will feel lighter and easier as you come to terms with all these feelings rather than trying to crush them or put them away! For me, it's about living life again with all my feelings.

GRIEF

I miss you…

Make a list of your experience of the different forms of grief and the effect on you.

Are there different forms of grief and even stages?

Yes, there are many: loss of job, partner, family member, health, death, pet and even the loss of a life you once had, moving home or country, children growing up and leaving home, change of job, promotion, divorce, or bodily changes …… With all of these, we usually attempt to move on much too quickly to start that new chapter or go in a new direction.

And it is important to remember your own self-worth in the face of others' detrimental opinion of you during your difficult times. You can take a hard knock if you are unable to withstand these opinions. One of these could be that, if you don't get back to 'normal' quickly enough, then you have failed and somehow not got back into living life again.

How can you support yourself (and others) when you (or they) are grieving?

Is grief a natural effect of loss?

Yes, and grief is an experience that needs support, love and witnessing rather than solutions. AND this view changes everything. When there is nothing else to hold onto, hold on to love. You cry and grieve because you can love, and it is okay to cry. Grief is the price we pay for love.

Some physical effects of grief can be over-eating/not eating, exhaustion, restlessness, lack of energy, sleeplessness or oversleeping, difficulty concentrating, cognitive changes, memory loss, confusion, anxiety and making decisions. While emotional effects can be loneliness, feeling worthless - 'there must be something wrong with me', regret, guilt, anger, numbness, detachment. Also, grief may have effects that go beyond its emotional toll as there is growing evidence linking it with e.g. heart disease (Karolinksa Institute, Sweden).

You need to be kind and take care of yourself. Your health can be affected too and some of the symptoms of, for example, your partner's ill-health, can seem like they become your symptoms.

How do you imagine you will feel when you know you can let go of your grief?
And how do you let go?

When will I stop grieving?

How long is a piece of string? I can't answer that as it varies for us all. I do know that grief can be seen by many as something to be solved. NO, it is a real experience. And what I do know is that society has learned the right words for responding to you – 'Rise above whatever you are feeling'. 'It all happens for a reason'. 'It's for the best' 'You're at stage xyz in the grieving process'. 'Look on the bright side'. Yes, all well-intentioned. BUT no. The words don't help anyone - only the person saying them! And you don't need to move on for the sake of others! It will happen in its own time, and the waiting can be difficult too.

How might we be different if, and when, we (you and others) are grieving?

Do we all grieve in the same way?

Kubler-Ross's 5 stages (denial, anger, bargaining, depression and acceptance) is a well- known model to have. BUT it is too simplistic and is seen nowadays as 'old hat' even if at the time it gave a template for us to hold on to. Sometimes people wait for each stage rather than focussing on what is happening to them in the moment. All the stages can even happen in the one day!!

You may be someone who has difficulty crying or showing your feelings and they may show up later unexpectedly. You could be doing something simple and quite suddenly you can feel the tears coming for no reason at all. You can even become furiously angry when it is totally inappropriate. And, of course, society doesn't want to see our anger so we push it away even when it may be totally appropriate.

One of the benefits of allowing yourself the gift of time, space and energy to focus on yourself is that you can re-connect with that deeper sense of gratitude for everything you do have. This can help to give you that breathing space.

If you have any regrets (who hasn't?) make a list of them and how you are dealing with them

What about regret?

There will always be regrets about what we should or could have done differently or better in our past. And when we admit truthfully to regret, we can then be open to 'that's how it was'. This can free us up to become more relaxed and engaged than we'd been in the past, say with our grandchildren or others.

Are you honestly able to own your relief (if you have any) - if only to yourself - and how does that make you feel?

What about a sense of relief?

This can also be a natural happening for those who have nursed or been involved with someone over a number of years. There is the relief that they are out of their pain and/or the relief from the pressure you may have been under in dealing with all the appropriate authorities, etc., which can definitely wear you down

22

25

LOSS

*Life is a one time offer,
use it well!*

What does Loss mean for you?

What do I mean by loss?

I'm using a definition of loss here as the end of a life you've always known but also the beginning of a new and different life. Life won't ever be the same. AND that's our fear.

Are you able to do this AND remember it may take a long while?

The reality of loss

Accepting the reality of loss is about accepting what is with strength. It is about knowing that everything will settle (all these thoughts, feelings and emotions) even if you don't understand it at the moment.

Remember, it is about you feeling safe and focussing on GRATITUDE again for what you do have and not for what you don't have!

In what ways do you deal with Loss and Change?

What about loss and change?

Like it or not, they are part of life – for good or bad. You thought you knew who you were before and now you don't. It is also difficult to let go, to surrender. We are called upon to trust that there will be a solution of sorts. To have the courage to allow things to unfold isn't easy as we are impatient to make things better.

Take your time and when ready reflect on what might happen for you in the future

What happens after loss?

You eventually slowly pick yourself up, get back on the saddle of your choice and move on! And this can be a rather glib response from me!! Sorry! But it is about eventually finding balance in life, where our mind, body and spirit begin to become whole again – not being content with only parts of our lives. It is about you being able to see, know you are okay and being aware of standing in another way of being. And also, that a new dawn is breaking.

What are the varying changes for you?

Are all losses equal?

No, and so the effects are different as we're all unique and to varying degrees. They cause physical and emotional change in us. And you now see a future that stretches out before you that doesn't look like you thought it would be! And that is both your challenge and excitement.

This is a good one to tussle with so give space to remember what is important to you

What is life all about?

May come up during this time. The turbulence of life at this time of loss and grief can bring up these big questions that we may not have addressed before. This is such a big question that people have been struggling with it for thousands of years. I can't give you a definitive answer (and don't know anyone who can) – not really - except those problems large or small, distractions, including our addictions, affairs and busyness keep us from facing the fact that we are all mortal. We are all going to die someday.

It's an act of courage to confront our fear of living, taking one day at a time and carrying on anyway. Few of us truly acknowledge and appreciate ourselves for doing this. Life isn't easy, let's be honest, and it is amazing when we realise that just keeping going can be an extraordinary feat in itself. It demonstrates the human resilience.

You need to remember that life is so much more than what happens to us. It is about how we respond to experiences, events and our immediate environment – failed relationships, loss of others, of health, of changes to our bodies, etc. But these aren't an indication that life has stopped (well maybe for a wee bit), and that we are permanently holding back or blocking ourselves from ever moving forward. We can do so much more if we recognise the opportunities for growth and better experiences that will be there for us WHEN WE ARE READY.

40

LONELINESS

Come to the edge, life said
They said, we are afraid.
Come to the edge: life pushed them
And they flew…

If any, Who or What provides that sense of belonging to you?

What is Loneliness?

It is so hard to admit to feeling lonely. Loneliness comes about because we come into this life ready to belong – to someone, something or somewhere we want to be seen by and connected with. Our need is to be held and to lean on someone who will let you do just that; to be comforted without judgement, seen, loved and appreciated. It is the feeling we get when our need for human contact and relationships (again, all part of the human condition we come into the world with) is unmet. It affects us all and it doesn't take me to tell you that it has a negative impact on our health!!

After 20 years of research, an American cardiologist found that no other factor – not diet, exercise, stress, smoking, genetics, drugs or surgery – affected our health and quality of life more than feeling loved and cared for. How interesting!! Another study done over 80 years found that the warmth of our relationships throughout life had the greatest impact on us.

Where, When and with Who do you feel lonely? And how do you deal with it?

How come I am lonely even within family/work/friends?

'There has to be something wrong with me' might be your thinking. You can't stop these lonely thoughts and feelings. Or perhaps you can, by acknowledging, giving space to them, including them, taking a few deep breaths and then be in life again – this takes a while.

Remember there is a difference between loneliness and choosing to be alone. Many of us feel lonely at some point in our life. It is perfectly normal and the shame you feel is part of life. It is all part of the spectrum of pain, sadness, fear, joy, love and faith. Loneliness goes much deeper than not having people to hang out with. It's about being invisible, not appreciated and feeling unloved. It can gnaw away at your sense of self-worth and belonging.

In my experience, these feelings can only be dealt with by focusing on something bigger than us or by having a conscious purpose in life to fulfil. To come out again from our safe haven and meet the world again is to heal our loneliness (inner and outer) from grief, from illness. To live again is to leave and let go of the excuses (lies we've told ourselves) as we're programmed not to risk ourselves, and to find ourselves alive once more. Do choose the opposite of becoming invisible – BE VISIBLE. AND remember, you can do it at your own pace.

Reflect on what ways you fulfil your basic need for Touch.

What about Touch?

We all need touch. Remember COVID? What a horrible time with the lack of touch – a hug, a hand not being held, a touch on our shoulder .... Nothing. This lack of touch brought our experience of loneliness even closer. It reminded us of our need for human contact in the light touch of another, through the trials of love, pain, loneliness, happiness of everyday life, through grief or recovery. This enables us to heal in order to be touched again in the right way, in a natural trusted invitation or simply by someone we care for.

The lack of touch means we disappear from ourselves and shrink away from ourselves and others. We are wired to be touched from when we come into the world until we die. And that need for physical contact remains throughout life. It plays a primary role in our development and in our physical and mental well-being. No wonder so many of us became depressed or at least 'out of sorts' when not having it! One way to bring touch into our life is to have massages, as well, of course, as the everyday hugging, kissing and shaking hands.

Why isn't it normal to give a hug, a kiss and to receive one back without words? Why can't we simply say 'I love you' without any sexual or other 'strings' attached? To allow ourselves simply to be held and allowed to cry enables us to feel our heart eased (balm for the soul) each time this happens. BUT it is a 'No Go' for society!! Many of us cannot do it as the pain is simply too much for us. When the mind can't bear the pain or the loss or the suffering (and we all have these feelings at times), when longing doesn't come in the form we wanted, we need solace or then our madness can take over.

What does being visible mean for you, and how do you express that?

Will I still be Visible as Me?

No, you'll have disappeared – you will have lost yourself; you will be overlooked for opinions/new jobs/promotion/on the dancefloor or anywhere else. And Yes, as you need to acknowledge that you are still here and alive. You have not disappeared. When we lose someone/something our identity goes in some way. Our other connections mean more to us, and we need them more than ever. Seek out those who will include you and don't go to things where you'll feel like a spare part. Put yourself in places or with people where you'll feel valued for who and what you are. The main issue is not to be invisible to yourself. When you are ready, I hope you will laugh at life as if it's some kind of cosmic joke! Hold it lightly.

An exercise I used to do with clients, was for them to look at themselves in the mirror and simply say, 'I See You' – it works. I still do it with myself too.

What shoe(s) are you choosing?

Where do I fit in now?

You won't - not in the old way – that shoe doesn't fit any more! It's up to you how you are even if you feel you are being forced back into shoes not of your choosing. Not finding a place for yourself in the world contributes to the feelings of being lost and depressed. Carl Jung said, 'Man cannot stand a meaningless life'. And it can be really tough to find a sense of meaning and purpose in life - and not only when we are in a place of loss. This is about the recognition that there will be a re-invention of you even if, for some, it may be only in a simple way. You won't be the same and that will be okay.

57

59

MADNESS

*Today is a gift and that's why
it's called the present*

How do you protect yourself from your Madness at these times?

My feelings of going mad are concerning me.

These feelings can come about because it could be said that we are out of contact with ourselves and so the balance of our mind gets disturbed. Hence our lives are affected. We don't know why we say or do things and they are usually silly! The shutter has opened up and our conscience no longer supports us. There is always some reason in our madness – usually protection from pain while it lets us hold onto life or love. My own loneliness was causing me to feel I was losing my mind – not a good place to be I can assure you.

As a psychologist, I am aware that grief and loss cause our minds and cognitive processes to go awry in so many unbelievable ways and we do feel 'mad'. It causes our memory to disappear and how to be and act socially. We can't understand what's being said, understand directions, forget names and anything you've done or have to do, nothing sticks when reading and one can go over the same thing time and time again, or find you've put things in the wrong places. ..... The inability to understand what others are doing or saying just doesn't make sense. You feel things more keenly. You can have times of unreality in public and feel like running out of the place. You can be hurling out things with no filter (particularly anger) and which are truly not appropriate with that person or at that time. You have literally been 'all shook up'. THAT'S THE DIFFERENCE!! It feels like you've stopped living and are going through the motions of your personal and professional life. ONCE AGAIN, YOU ARE NOT MAD – YOU ARE EXPERIENCING GRIEF AND LOSS – AND THAT'S THE DIFFERENCE.

In what ways do you avoid/face your pain?

Facing the Reality of Pain

It has been said that the only real pain is the avoidance of pain! Nobody truly wants to face the reality of their pain – not really. It is much too scary so most of us would rather stick our heads in the sand and hope whatever it is will change all on its own. Our thoughts are usually along the lines of 'I'll wake up again and life will be the same as before'! Our hearts get broken in untold ways that can't be fixed. We do get better at learning to bear witness to our own and others' hurts. We learn how to survive all parts of love, even the difficult ones. Most of us spend our lives trying vainly to avoid loss, vulnerability, fear and heartbreak with our vulnerability being the main one.

What rules to you have (consciously or unconsciously) that say life ought to be fair, and where do they come from?

Isn't life unfair?

Of course, it is. It is all too hard, and we are disenchanted from the beginning as we become aware of the reality of life.

AND who said it was going to be fair in the first place???

When and how do you give yourself permission to let go?

What about my vulnerability or my anger or these tears that I have no control over?

And this can happen any time anywhere! Let them all BE by allowing them to be free even if that's only in your own home or with anyone you trust and sometimes it can be anywhere.

Try to find trusted people or even one person who allows you to BE however you are when you need to just 'be'. As we will never know ourselves fully so how can others think they really know and can judge us? We need to feel or express our hurt or our anger in whatever way suits us. For me, one way is to get it out of my body i.e. move so I don't let it weigh me down. You need to forgive yourself by being compassionate and kind to yourself so you can live with your vulnerability.

In what ways can you allow your reality in?

I am under pressure to be happy

Stop sugar-coating your sh*t for the outside world. Yes, because others care about you and want to see you are happy as they cannot deal with your pain. Some simply don't know how to listen as others' pain touches them and that is very uncomfortable, so they want you to be happy for their sake!

It's time for us all to be more honest with our vulnerability and to stop hiding how it really is for us. Will your problems go away if you are happy? NO, not always. So DO and BE what you want to do and be and don't give out what is expected of you. It is also okay to hide your unhappiness as YOU will be choosing to do this. And when you are ready, have the courage to embrace whatever is going on for you as you have that power. Remember being happy or sad are two sides of the same coin – life.

Some Other Issues Affecting Us

*Changing your attitude to life,
will change your life*

The following are some reactions and/or thoughts you might be having about that gaping hole of Loss. You may be having others so write them in the journal part.

What conscious or unconscious reactions have you/ are you experiencing?

Are there any conscious reactions from others to your Loss, Loneliness & Madness?

Yes, again all the platitudes others say! These kind of obvious responses, for example, are to be told 'Get over it', 'Remember the good times'. But you don't, not really 'get over it'. Remember, it says more about them! Of course, people want you to take away their hurt – make them feel better – as that is just how we are. And yet, change happens as you gradually construct a new reality around your loss, loneliness and madness. And they will still be with the core of you. Sometimes you will simply laugh at yourself even if it's just an inner smile.

Something else that can happen is that People don't want to speak to you about what's happening for you. This can be how it is even with old, close friends. It is understandable as you are a mirror to what could happen to them. And, as I have said earlier, it can be too painful for them because they love you and they'd rather mouth platitudes and move on to other things. They have done what is expected of them as they go through the expected motions of response and so can feel good!

How do you avoid your feelings of fear so that they don't overwhelm or consume you?

What are we all afraid of?

FEAR – knowing that we are all going to die some time. Our shame and embarrassment must be hidden. We mustn't show our vulnerability or be REAL as society doesn't want this of us. Some other fears are – of failure, success, rejection, disappointment, or even unconscious fears we didn't know we had! What frees us is Courage (Coeur = the Heart). This isn't the absence of fear but the willingness to break through the limitations we put on ourselves.

My stance in the past - long gone - has been that my life hasn't had any meaning, that I've lived in vain, that my existence hasn't made any difference to anyone or anything. All untrue. But this kind of thinking can drive any of us to be busy, busy, busy. Or even to give up on life and settle in our own little comfort box and so we don't connect with others or life. BUT the thing is that we become more visible when we allow in our courage, vulnerability and compassion for ourselves and others and take this into life. Remember, healing is a process and won't happen overnight so take it easy as you may be in it for the long haul.

Reflect on the fact that you have Choice

Do I have to be polite to all and sundry while I am feeling like this?

F**k Hell – NO. Haven't you heard of CHOICE? You choose how you want to respond to others' enquiries and to their issues. You can care for and respond to the right people and ignore others in your own way.

List your judgements and reflect on how they make you feel

I've difficulty being non-judgemental especially at this time, of those just going through the motions of responding to my loss.

No problem at all so don't worry. I don't know anyone who is free of judgements so let it go. You can see people as they really are to you and then choose how to be towards them.

How do you react to change — body, feelings, mind?

Once this is all over, will I change?

No and Yes. NO, you won't, as the lure of your comfort zone has too big a hold on you. You will just sit and moan and groan but not do much as your FEAR is too big. You will feel guilty when you are enjoying yourself as guilt is part of the human condition – guilt for all you didn't do while forgetting all that you did do. At some point you need to acknowledge that there may always be some guilt, so simply acknowledge and include it.

And then for others, YES you will change, and you can relish it rather than mourn the change, and then get on with life. Time can help as our healing does take time – two steps forward and ten backwards!!

Take time out and listen to yourself and your dreams

I am still saying 'Is this it?'

NO – there will be a little step forward for you, I hope. This can seem like new territory for you, and you can relish it rather than mourn the change. What about reflecting on those dreams you had when you were little AND go do them!!

Time to draw on your Courage and see what happens

Should I take risks and make life my own?

Yes! You might do it in your head but will hold back in real life as it's too risky to listen to the longings of your heart. Then you will beat yourself up afterwards. Take that risk!!

What do you hear when you listen to yourself? Now go do it!

What can I do?

Sometimes all you can do is simply live with your losses, your loneliness and your madness!! Sometimes there just isn't an answer – there's no right or wrong way - that's the way it is. Some find they are drawn to spirituality or religion or re-connect with their faith (in whatever form) as a deeper way of sustaining themselves. Some re-kindle their love of learning and open up to new ideas. Some find a new love of nature and all that means for them. Some re-connect with what used to give them feelings of joy. Some find the groups that appeal to all aspects of themselves. There is a big, wide world out there, so it is over to you.

And remember to listen to yourself by going inside to your heart as that's where you'll find the simplicity of grace with ease (peace of mind).

97

RECONNECTION

*Go with your dreams
and reality will be kind to you*

How have you lost yourself over time?

How do we re-connect to ourselves, to our heart, our soul?

In the past, I had a family, working life, was creative, and wrote blogs and books. At the time of writing, this book was all about re-igniting with these, and my re-connection with myself. It is a step forward in my sharing with you. I decided I was not going to wait around for a publisher so I connected with people from the past and decided to do it this way. And I am still looking for my next step.

I would also say to you that the re-connection is about finding all the ways that make you joyful. Sometimes you hide yourself from yourself. You are not willing to own YOURSELF by only showing the world what they want to see (or you think that). Then one day you realise you don't know who you are any more. You've forgotten YOU! You've forgotten your inner spark and the gifts you can offer life. What would you re-ignite and bring back into your life?

I would say that this is your life's purpose: To re-discover those talents or gifts so that you can freely show and share the connection to yourself, your heart and your soul.

And come home to YOU.

Not only come home to you but feel your way into a newly emergent you.

I SEE YOU.

GO WELL xx

ABOUT THE AUTHOR

Irene is one of those women who has been there, done that and got the 't' shirt over her many years.

She is originally from Glasgow, lived in Essex, worked in London and mainland Europe (particularly Stockholm) drawing on her personal and professional background.

Irene now lives in Northern Ireland where she has written this third book, and enjoys the company of a few (very few) kind, caring, humorous and generous friends.

Her life has been one of: 'Life is what happens to you while you are busy making other plans' and so it goes on.